Pioneering Female Authors
in Egypt and the Levant

An Introduction into the Origins of the Arabic Novel

Hoda Thabet

Contents

Chapter Three
Intercultural and Inter-Traditional Understanding............. 77

Chapter One
Arabic Women's Authorship

Reading as a Form of Resistance

I continued to be a voracious reader and this voracity heightened my sense of deprivation from academic studies. Someone with high ambitions comes to harbor feelings of bitterness, arising from that vacuum left in the soul by being deprived when young of the chance to study. She becomes a bookworm (Tuqan, *A Mountainous Journey* 126, cited by Ashour 227)[1].

It may be argued that both reading and writing are forms of resistance, creating spaces in which to re-imagine gender roles and intersections of power. Fiction and non-fiction hold equally important places, but the novel may stand as the pre-eminent form for the exploration of transitions in identity and being, and the metamorphoses that may be possible. Therefore, the exercise of reading and writing anything other than texts approved by the dominant authorities must always be seditious in the context of a repressive social order. Grace argues that

---

[1]See also Terri DeYoung's essay "Love, Death and the Ghost of Al-Khansa: The Modern Female Poetic Voice in Fadwa Tuqan's Elegies for her brother Ibrahim" on pp. 45-75 in *Tradition, Modernity and Post-Modernity in Arabic Literature: Essays in Honor of Professor Issa J. Boullata*, edited by Kamal Abdel-Malek and Wael Hallaq (published by Brill in 2000) on Fadwa Tuqan's poetry, the Western stereotype of voiceless Arabic women, aspects of the 1948 and 1967 conflicts, and the long shadow of the early female poet, Al-Khansa.

[w]riting remains for Arab women a key means of subverting dominant hegemonies and reasserting agency, a means of voicing their 'silenced' narratives. ... Risking censorship, slander, or possible imprisonment, the Arab woman writer is a dissident crossing into the male space of language .(185)

This researcher suggests that, while reading forbidden or disapproved texts does not always carry the same dangers as writing them, elements of subversion and risk are involved in both.

In his analysis of the novel, Georg Lukács states that the loss of the immanence of meaning in life and the symbolic forms traditionally used to encode and decode resulted in changing literary forms and crisscrossed genres. "That is why tragedy, although changed, has nevertheless survived in our time with its essential nature intact, whereas the epic had to disappear and yield its place to an entirely new form: the novel" (2). If novels seek to establish new symbology and new ways to negotiate identity and meaning, the work of Joseph Campbell has in some respects added to Lukács's analysis by posing the problem of the loss of myths that are central to our consciousness, being and becomingness, or personal and social development.

Campbell suggests that science and modernity have destroyed or diminished important metaphorical ways for us to perceive ourselves, our parents, society and our passage through life, with the changing identities and roles that progress entails. Misunderstanding metaphors as literal truths has permitted their disintegration in the face of seeming contradictions from science and modernity, resulting in the dissolution of identity and psycho-social structure.

Women, marginalized throughout history, have willingly stepped into the liminal, transitional spaces generated by the disintegration of former belief systems in order to create new meanings. Novels may well be the form in which both writers and readers can engage in deconstructing the social logic of oppression, and search for, conceptualize and project new gendered identities, new symbols, and new principles to understand better the transitions, mutations and fluidity of modern identity.

Novels were ordinarily released in serialized form through journals. The explosion of the new "Arab women's press," principally in Egypt, Syria and Lebanon, suggests a strong demand for women's writing and growing freedom of expression, education and intellectual pursuits. Bouthaina Shaaban emphasizes the critical importance of the women's press, not only in demarginalizing and debating women's issues, but as a key component in the Arabic media as a whole. "Any assessment of Arab (or, for that matter, global) women's literature cannot be done without evaluating the Arab women's press, which was for half a century the major platform for Arab women writers" (10).

Hind Nawfal, a Syrian living in Alexandria, founded *Al-Fatat* in 1892[2]. She was followed six years later by Alexandra Afernuh, who founded *Anis al-Jalis* and selected contributors from Europe and other parts of the world to document the position of women in their locales. In all, women owned, wrote, edited and published more than 25 magazines and journals before the First World War (Shaaban 11). Although readership figures are not readily available, it seems probable that there was a sufficient readership to support the large numbers of magazines and journals being produced by and for women as a form of resistance.

Yet women's ability to partake of such literary freedoms often seems to have been due to individual rather than general circumstances, and subject to chance, social standing, the whims of immediate male family members, and other capricious factors beyond a woman's control. At the same time as women's education was being lauded as a cornerstone for modernization and national liberation, people shouted at the ten-year old writer Anbara Salam Al Khalidi (1897-1988) to go home when she was on her way to lessons (al-Id 15).

The disparity between the ideals of self-determination, freedom and modernization preached in journals, and the rather less rosy reality

---

[2]The complete collection was published in 2006 by the Women and Memory Forum.

women endured in real life, is illustrated by a daunting incident in Anbara Salam Al Khalidi's young life.

> The day that Anbara Salam stood on the podium to speak, wearing her full veil, one of the men spoke up: 'What an inauspicious disgrace! How can her father allow his daughter to speak before a gathering of men? By God, by God, I'd like to shoot her and spare the world from her'. (al-Id 15)

Perhaps typical of the contradictions of the time, that confrontation occurred in Beirut, a city "well situated to be the link between East and West, a free space for cultural dialogue, open to the West and its rationalist civilization" (14). Anbara Salam al-Khalidi accepted the challenge, and—refusing to be intimidated—went on to participate in intellectual, political and social discourse.

She added to the body of important translations during what Jurji Niqula Baz called the "feminine renaissance" of the late 19th and early 20th centuries by translating the *Iliad* and the *Odyssey*, wrote tirelessly and influentially about women's education, and later published her memoirs, *A Tour of Memories of Lebanon and Palestine*. Lebanese autobiography is a somewhat *rara avis* that, "more closely resembles writing about reality and its manifestations than expressions of the female interior self in its particularity and its stifled intimacy" (al-Id 55). This absence of the personal in an essentially personal form may have been a defensive device to deflect the prevalent criticisms that women were self-obsessed and were better suited to write about their thoughts and emotions than more important matters; it may also have served to protect her from personal attacks.

As we shall see, some of the criticisms leveled at women's writing were not only narrowly phallocentric, bigoted, unreasonable and dismissive; they were also illogical even within their own logical structure. It is important to understand something of the environment in which these early modern women writers worked. It may be argued that society has evolved, but that the attitudes and patriarchal social logic that were prevalent during those times are still relevant today.

Writing on the Edge

Does anything more than danger stimulate our creativity? And does anything threaten our creativity more than danger?

~Nawal el-Saadawi

In their joint study of Syrian women writers, Subhi Hadidi and Iman al-Qadi noted the extraordinary accomplishments of Mary 'Ajami born in Damascus in 1888 (d. 1965). As with other writers of the renaissance or revival period, her work touched many spheres; she was not content simply to found a magazine, *The Bride*, to publish, to edit and to write. While not a novelist, her writing was groundbreaking on both artistic and social levels. Even to sustain the magazine during the period of Ottoman repression and censorship required an uncommon degree of energy and dedication, but she achieved considerably more than that. Hers was no passionless intellect: "It is said that she demanded an interview with Jamal Pasha, the Ottoman tyrant who ruled Syria with iron, fire, and gallows, to ask for amnesty for detained nationalists" (60). She visited prisons and uncovered human rights violations suffered by detainees, inviting reprisal but continuing to publish and take grave risks in her struggle for the freedom of both men and women. Thus, 'Ajami practiced resistance with both pen and body, reaching beyond the boundaries of power and discipline that produced what Foucault called "subjected and practiced bodies, 'docile' bodies" (138-9). Her engagement with power was intellectual, personal, and physical.

'Ajami's "pro-women" attainments are remembered, but perhaps it would be more relevant to memorialize her pro-human accomplishments. Indeed, Subhi Hadidi takes care to highlight the fact that 'Ajami emancipated men as well as women (60). When Jurji Niqula Baz (known as the Supporter of Women) wrote her biography in celebration of her 25th year as a writer, he described both her painstaking methods of research and writing and her willingness to change (Booth 83).[3] In the face of real danger, 'Ajami's courage and readiness to experience transition and transformation as agent and as an object, set her apart as a special combination of author and leader. 'Ajami's writing was a form of resistance that required personal bravery, even audacity, which was seldom associated with women; it argued eloquently for a change in the inherited perceptions that burdened gendered identity and roles.

Her personal experience was linked to the political and feminist spaces she occupied, but her arguments (and actions) were commonly aimed towards a comprehensive feminism that targeted

---

[3]Jurji Niqula Baz should get special mention for documenting the lives of women writers of his day, and founding a magazine, *al Hasna* or *Fair Lady*, to be "the voice of feminine renaissance" (Zeidan 25).

inequity towards both men and women, recognizing that, as long as either suffers, both must also suffer. In such an approach people will only develop to their full potential together rather than at the expense of one another. Her sense of the personal process of *becomingness* was cooperative and essentially non-adversarial. 'Ajami, was undaunted by adversarial stances against abuses of power, but she tended to include the misery of both men and women in her writing.

miriam cooke notes that 'Ajami's literary club, founded in 1922, was neither the first nor the last in Syria, and owed nothing to the French tradition of *salons* presided over by intelligent, highly cultured women such as Madame de Staël. Such socio-cultural assemblies were integral to Arab society; the difference in the modern era was that, instead of meeting in a home, men and women met in a public place (54-55). Unafraid of criticizing the Ottoman and then French occupations, 'Ajami continued to have an impact on women's writing throughout her active life; she went on to found the Nur al-Fayha' (Damascus Light) Society and the Women's Cultural League, helping to ensure that important connections were made in the lively interchanges to foster human—and not simply feminist—development in Syria. 'Ajami's living definition of feminism was far-sighted and remains relevant today.

Arabic Women's Writing and the Growth of Modernity

Since this book involves modern Arabic writing, it may be useful to mention the concept of modernity in the context of post-colonial women authors. In Kamran Rastegar's discussions of textual transactions between Arabic, Persian and English literatures during the nineteenth century, he deals with the difficult and elusive definition of modernity. This study addresses women's writing in the late nineteenth and early twentieth centuries in Syria, Lebanon and Egypt. Rastegar tries to avoid a Eurocentric view of modernity by defining it as "the very act of change" and "going so far as to charge it with a central role in the conceptualization of the sublime" (12). His premise is valuable here: it is in the space between the sublime and the temporal that "culture gains autonomy from the clutch of religious and monarchical systems of legitimation" (12). It is this autonomy which we view as modernity in this study.

Elsadda describes the co-evolution of women's writing and modernity, and the "particularity" that distinguishes women's writing from men's, as resulting from complex, changing relationships between perceptions of self and Other, the critical and popular reception of writings, the appreciation and affirmation of certain writers and their ideas, and the norms and standards by which women's writing is appraised (101). She argues that the difference in women's creative writing is positional and contextual. It is not physiological, rather it is, "determined by women's locus in the symbolic cultural order and their relationship with it" (101).

While the interrelationships Elsadda describes are of great importance, the work of some writers, such as el-Saadawi, is so embodied—informed by and pervaded by both the female and male body—as voice, identity and subject/object, that the biological cannot easily be excluded. However, Elsadda interestingly connects the relationships she describes with the backlash women underwent for daring to try to advance both their own cause and that of their country. Unfortunately, this is not mere historical artifact. Women became a "locus for conflicts" and were to blame for many issues at that time, and continue to be right up to the present day (101).

> This context produced much writing that addresses the status of women in society, linking women's 'backwardness' with social backwardness and blaming women for their inferior status. In contrast, we do not find the same amount of writing about men's backwardness, and no connections are made between the backwardness of society and specific elements of the male character or men's lives. As such, women became the Other, inscribed and invested with all the latent problems and taboos; they were the mirror in which men looked to avoid facing the self .(101)

Elsadda portrays the almost overwhelming attention given in magazines and newspapers to the position, duties and rights of women in relation to increasing nationalism.

The intertwining of feminist and nationalist issues was a mixed blessing. "This interest in the cause of women had a significant, positive impact on women's general status, although there is a clear tendency to blame women and hold them responsible for society's backwardness and, thus, the burden of its advancement" (9). Writing later in Syria, Walid Sakakini also lamented the palpable shift of blame onto women for national, cultural, political backwardness.

> It pains me that in the 1940s, even as Arab women are shaking off their lethargy, learning and advancing, entering universities, and contributing to society, they are still accused of inadequacy and backwardness. Our most prominent writers blame them for every fault ... (209)

Women are still experiencing such unfairly allocated blame. Ghada Samman recently echoed this view, criticizing those who hold Arab women responsible for failing to modernize in the Western mode: "It is better that we investigate the reasons for the Arab woman's backwardness instead of returning her to her chains in the cave and saying that she is only fit for its darkness" (Samman cited by Wayne 574).

Added to this burden of responsibility, while being deprived of commensurate power, are the dimensions of colonialism and self-colonialism—specifically what Lila Abu-Lughod, Edward Said and others cite as the colonial view of the "backwardness of the East," internalized by colonized men and projected onto women as the source of their own socio-political deficiencies and lack of development (perhaps at best, the blame should be shared). Thus, the alliance with nationalism, the very tool of empowerment for women, was the weapon used against them. The subversion of the necessity for the simultaneous liberation of women and men was a severe disappointment for certain women writers, some of whom later chose to retire from political activism and even stopped publishing their work.

Some women seem to have shared this sense of responsibility for backwardness, but with a significant difference. Zaynab Fawwaz blamed women for "seeing themselves and their lives from the perspectives and opinions of men...so that they came to recognize themselves only through them" (cited by Fawwaz Traboulsi 16). At a time when women spoke of their natural limitations and accepted the male-dominated paradigm, her observations were both acute and farsighted. It would be decades before Simone Beauvoir echoed some of Zaynab Fawwaz' conclusions.

With assumed birthdates varying from 1846 to 1860 (d. 1914), much of Zaynab Fawwaz's early life is mysterious, including her migration from Lebanon to Egypt, and is suggestive of a deep unconventionality in her personal relations with men. She was a pioneer; publishing essays in

Hasan Husni Pasha al-Tuwayrani's *al-Nil* during the 1890's advocating the social benefits of progressive women's rights. Her extensive documentation of the lives and achievements of some 456 women, from various eras and places, became a key text for many women writers, including, "Malak Hifni Nasif, and especially the owners of and contributors to women's journals, who drew inspiration from it or reprinted large segments..." (Elsadda 105).

If imitation is the sincerest form of flattery, the fact that portions of her biographical dictionary were sometimes reprinted without attribution, and frequently used with little change, may tend to confirm her influence on other writers. Begun in 1891, four years later the Bulaq Press published Zaynab Fawwaz' *Scattered Pearls in the Lives of the Harem Dwellers*, also rendered as *Scattered Pearls in Generations of Mistresses of Seclusion*, which Booth calls a "geographically and diachronically wide-ranging dictionary", and was a significant marker in the appropriation of men's writing by women and the advancement of Arab women (120).

Booth has produced a brief but important biography of this remarkable woman.[4] In her introduction to *Scattered Pearls,* Fawwaz stated that what prompted her to write it was that she could not

---

[4] In *Essays in Arabic Literary Biography 1350-1850* Vol. III, ed. Roger Allen. Wiesbaden: Harrassowitz, pp. 93-98. See also *An Introduction to Arabic Literature* by Roger Allen, Cambridge University Press, pp. 46-48.

find a single Arabic book devoted to the manifold and significant accomplishments of women through the ages, so she set about rectifying this omission. The fact that no one had previously noticed this literary and historical *lacuna* (or no one had felt strongly enough about it) gives some indication of the sort of impact her work must have had. Redefining history in women's terms is a remarkable project and suggests a strong awareness of and drive for women's *becomingness*. That is, she provided examples not only to re-inscribe the past, but also to change the future: women must be free to experience their own being and their potential to become. Booth noted another aspect of the "collective impact" of these biographies. Showing women from ancient to modern times who had demonstrated intellectual prowess, were respected and capable teachers, who were judicious and astute in ruling large dominions, and who reached for important social objectives broke down the "notion of essential or 'natural' gender roles" (97).

In the framework of its time, fostering understanding of and appreciation for the achievements, courage and perseverance of women by reversing the masculine tradition of biography may have been more far subversive than it may seem today. "Women writing about women" has become commonplace since the time Fawwaz first conceived of it and then dared to do it. Biographical literature has a long and prestigious history in Arabic, one of the earliest extant being *The Great Book of Generations*, a vast, multi-volume, invaluable work of both apocryphal and factual narratives by Muhammad Ibn Sa`id (784- 845 CE). "By using the word *tabaqat* in her title, Fawwaz declared a generic linkage to a venerable Arabo-Islamic tradition of biographical writing ..." (Booth 120)[5].

Fawwaz' efforts did not go unnoticed. Her subversion of the masculine form was successful and triggered a new trend of "women writing about women," followed by Qadriyya Husayan, May Ziyada, Labiba Hashim and others (Elsadda 106, Booth 35). Juxtaposing women from East and West tended to decenter both. Further, Elsadda notes that, "Zaynab Fawwaz's writings had an enormous impact on the newspapers and magazines of the time." This study concentrates on works by Arabic women writers that enjoyed a large readership and may be assumed to be influential; Arabic women's authorship may have a longer and richer history than is generally realized.

Although Fawwaz continually tests the borders of power, even when she is writing about women who were rulers, she seemed to stress domesticity and morality as imperative and exemplary feminine qualities. All of the women included in her biographies were examples to be followed, and all were paragons of virtue. Fawwaz maintained the definitions of virtue, chastity and homelike comforts

---

[5] One of the volumes of *The Great Book of Generations* is dedicated to women, which was translated by Aisha Abdurrahman Bewley and published as *The Women of Madina* by Taha Publishers, 1995.

that served male-dominated society. Booth argues, however, that this was not the "discourse of containment" that it may seem at first glance. Fawwaz emphasized the importance of domesticity as a strategy to help her works obtain a wide acceptance, and did not view the domestic as the exclusive role for women.

The public debate between Fawwaz and the Lebanese woman writer Hana Kasbani Kurani who attacked Fawwaz's ideas of women in the public sphere (in which other notable figures joined, such as `Arif al-Zayn) on this very point supports this reading. Kurani had written a newspaper article stating that, "women cannot work outside the home while at the same time fulfilling the duties incumbent upon her to serve her husband and children" (cited by Wayne 312). Wayne explains that Fawwaz and Kurani took oppositional stances. Fawwaz made an "elegant riposte": women are intellectually equal to men, excelling in fields as diverse as mathematics, philosophy and engineering, and are "entitled to pursue equivalent avenues of professional endeavors as their male counterparts" (312).

Booth suggests that the strategy of emphasizing the domestic became more widely practiced in the 1920's and later, as a result of the repercussions against women who were politically active. Booth sees female biography in a collective light, not minimizing the fact of contradictions and diversity, but attempting to articulate and transmit a modern, proud, and capable identity for women that included a fusion of East and West, and which enjoyed a presence, "across a range of journals and over a period of time" (xix). Fawwaz' place in this broadly-felt presence is prominent.

Although controversial, she was also prolific and popular: she had written a play in 1893, *Love and Fidelity*, which is conspicuous for its rarity in a time of sparse dramatic production; an historical novel in 1899, *Fine Consequences, or Radiant Ghada*; and in 1905, an historical adventure-romance tale, *King Cyrus* (105). Writing can be conceived of as a monologic activity, however, Fawwaz' active participation in public debate (as mentioned, for example, with Hana Kasbani Kurani, who had written that women were created by God to raise children) suggests that for Fawwaz, writing was highly discursive, public and dialogic in nature. Evidently, for her the reader was an integral part of the text. The nature of *Scattered Pearls* and that fact it was invited to participate in one the biggest events of its kind in the latter half of the nineteenth century—the 1893 Chicago Exposition—also demonstrates that information, ideas and inspiration traveled between the East and West, and not merely from West to East.

Fawwaz's gendered manipulation of history was perhaps more far-reaching than may at first appear. Threads of diaspora, exile and alienation seem to be laced through both Fawwaz's fiction and non-fiction. Colonialism, the sense of being an alien in one's own country, conflict, displacement and dispersal have complicated the already intricate politics of identity for those diverse and disparate women known under the convenient umbrella term of Arab women writers. Al-Id insists that Fawwaz, like other Lebanese writers of the pioneering times, focused on "local Lebanese content" (18).

The background for *Fine Consequences, or Radiant Ghada* is a power struggle amongst the ruling class in southern Lebanon; the foreground is comprised of a microcosmic family struggle amongst ordinary people. It is placed in Jawal Abil, her place of birth, and contains autobiographical elements. Her uniquely Arabic literary devices have been criticized unjustly against Western standards—for example, her excessive use of ornament, her linguistic virtuosity, and the interruption of narrative flow with poetry or comments. These distinctive and formerly cherished traditional features of Arabic literature may have been instrumental in causing her work to become somewhat undervalued as being of greater historical than literary interest.

Al-Id further notes that Fawwaz uses a linking technique reminiscent of that used by Shahrazad (or Scheherazade), in which she "links her beginnings with where she left off, as if the blank whiteness of the paper between chapters is the white brightness of day between one night and the next. In both white spaces, there is silence and an absence: the absence of women until they resume speaking" (18).

The conceptual or emotional connection with Shahrazad suggests that Fawwaz also has skillfully spun tales in order to affirm her existence and experience life. Reminding us of the unwritten heritage of women's stories, al-Id points out that, "women seem to have a knack for storytelling and that this orality is a vestige of this ancient mode" (18).

Al-Id's reading of Fawwaz is perceptive, yet it could be inaccurate to delimit Fawwaz's work as being tied to local interests. Her work is versatile and experimental, and simultaneously local and universal. Freely adapting raw, new material, selecting traditional material at will, and knowingly using personal history combined with fiction, her work reveals an authorial self-confidence that is striking at this early stage of women's writing. Six years before *Fine Consequences, or Radiant Ghada* (also called, *A Happy Ending*) she had written a play set in Iraq—a bold act in a religious and social environment that did not encourage drama.

Drama is outside the scope of this book, but, as perhaps the most public art form, it offers a rich field, laden with transcultural issues and public debate. The fact that Fawwaz chose to participate in such a literary form is interesting in itself. All the while, she also produced feminist essays and strongly promoted the importance of women's entrance to the workplace for economic independence, as well as the essential intellectual equality (if not superiority) of women.

Booth maintains that Fawwaz was not an innovator, "[b]ut she dared to put conventional forms to new uses, and old usages to new effects. ... She dared to challenge other writers in the public forum of the press, unveiling her name and her views if not her face" (98).

Fawwaz understood and used both traditional Arabic literary forms and topics, and the newer Western works, from which she was able to select and combine; hence, her work—dealing with women's, socio-political, and religious issues—stands at an important transitional juncture in women's writing, modernity and Arabic literature as a whole.

Mervat F. Hatem reminds us that a custom of the time, namely including the names of noted authors who endorsed a book or journal, was especially problematic for women. Literary circles were, of course, a male province. Aisha Ismat Taymur, an erudite and established writer, had a high reputation and generously lent her name to endorse and help to launch the careers of unknown authors, such as Zaynab Fawwaz and Hind Nawfal. In turn, the new authors were able to initiate a younger generation to Taymur's work.

This process of banding together acted as a kind of resistance to the segregation of women from the center of discourse and its power, effectively demonstrating that women writers, though few in number, were a genuine intellectual force rather than a fad. "The resulting small sisterhood of women allowed the few women writers and/or those interested in women's education to contribute to the development of new forms of social solidarity among women" (Hatem 199).

Reclaiming Lost Intellectual History

Gaining a fuller understanding of women's roles in the history of thought is an important feminist objective. Perhaps more fundamental an influence on women's Arabic writing than that of Fawwaz is the work of Aisha Ismat Taymur (1840–1902). Hatem details the impact of her work, particularly in light of developing gender relations and nation building, as well as the reasons for its subsequent misassessment and underappreciation. Ornate, evocative and mind-stretching wordplay is not merely an antique device but as integral to an understanding of her work as, for example, the same feature in the work of John Donne.

Hatem contends that the narrow scope of modernist readings of Taymur's *oeuvre* misses not only much of its delicate resonance and eloquence, but also much of its deeper meaning. She argues persuasively for a new look at Taymur's relevance and at the power of her discourse, which is not diminished by its gracefulness. In contradistinction to prevailing modernist criteria, which have classified nineteenth century literary output, as either traditional or modern in a linear narrative that searched for an abrupt forma and thematic break that signaled the successful modernization of the nation and its literary forms of expression, Taymur's works combined elements of continuity and change reflected in the development of hybrid writing styles and literary forms coupled with introduction of novel perspectives couched in deceptively familiar social-political themes (195).

Elsadda concurs, pointing out that May Ziyada, who attributed what she perceived to be Taymur's traditionalism to "imitativeness and imperfect poetic vision" and criticized Taymur for speaking with the voice of a man, failed to understand this "important beginning that combined the old and the new" (105). As a member of the transitional generation of women writers on the cusp of modernity, Taymur had roots in a fast-disappearing world while reaching into new worlds, but the winds of change "blew away the important history of the beginning of women's writing in the modern age" (105).

Suffering from its position outside the dominant critique, her work displays a linguistic facility and adroitness which invites admiration and criticism for precisely the same reasons. Reclaiming part of the intellectual history of Taymur's era may also help to ground the complicated and continuing negotiation between feminism, modernity and national identity.

Elsadda proposes Taymur as the first experimenter with the modern Arabic novel and cites May Ziyada's 1922 biography of Taymur in which she saw "the spark of modern fiction" in *Meeting after Separation* (103). Another important work, Taymur's *The Mirror of Contemplation* (1892) proposed new readings of the Qur'an's *ayat* regarding the conditional, contingent nature of man's mastery over woman, which were taken seriously enough to have provoked, "important responses from Shaykh ʿAbdallah al-Fayyumi, a member of the ulama class[6], and ʿAbdallah al-Nadim, one of the leading nationalist writers of this period" (Hatem 4). Responses ranged from antagonistic to supportive, and it was not merely an erudite controversy. Taymur used an "Islamic-rationalist approach" to analyze the impact of developing national community on gender relations and to criticize colonial modernization (Hatem 115).

Fully seven years before Qasim Amin's *The Liberation of Women*, Hatem notes the early influence of this debate during a landmark year in Egyptian politics. "The public debate that Taymur's views triggered in 1892 represented what should be legitimately considered as the first national public debate on gender issues and concerns" (4). Her philosophy that called for an alternative course in the development of a new social logic deserves attention, and will be briefly analyzed here.

Mervat F. Hatem's original and very welcome study brings to light the sophistication in Taymur's understanding of some of the most critical and complex issues of her day and her vision for a way forward. Taymur foresaw that the nationalistic changes taking place would affect the manner in which men exercised control over

---

[6] A class of Islamic scholars, historically possessing considerable power.

women. The "redefinition of the relations that men had with each other as economic and political actors" would also result in shifts in the power structure in which women were subjugated; such shifts would not necessarily be benevolent towards women.

She was perhaps the only woman to have articulated the concern about how the traditional patriarchal society was evolving into a modern society, one that was still patriarchal, but in different and perhaps more insidious ways. Hatem convincingly contends that Taymur was very much aware that such changes, "were affecting the definition of women's membership in the nation" (195). In older patriarchal societies, kinship defined the power that each man had over women in the family, but not over women outside the family as a group. The nation as a horizontal fraternity relied very heavily on the discursive power that men as a group had over women as a group (195).

Therefore, the increased control over women was not balanced by a sense of responsibility for women. Male privilege could grow without check, unless women could redefine masculinity and, by extension, leadership. Taymur is sensitive to the power relations at the core of the feminist project that seeks to understand the origin and character of women's subordination. Although not fully articulated, her work suggests a micro-political concept of the operation of power that echoes Foucault's understanding of power, "as circulating throughout the social body rather than emanating from the top down" (Sawicki 164).

The newly developing "horizontal fraternity" and the means whereby women could avoid, subvert, or eliminate new forms of domination and victimization were her major concerns. She was always ready to frame gender relations within the terms of political alignments, clearly perceiving analogies in the male-dominated hierarchies of family and government, and supported less hierarchical and more democratic forms of government (Hatem 196). Her sense of woman as a whole being, capable of full self-realization, put her at deep variance with majority thought at the time.

Taymur was one of the few writers of her time to be able to rise above dichotomous oppositions and attempt a synthesis as a very real alternative to the tired choices revolving around modernism and traditionalism that still plague many societies. She advocated "a synthetic reform agenda whose goal was to put modernity into the service of Islamic society and its distinct forms of expression" (195).

Thus her socio-political project rejected deadlocked oppositional arguments in order to embrace a more complicated but potentially far more rewarding dialogue aimed at constructing a more coherent and egalitarian social order. She had no desire to subjugate either Islamic values or modernization. Hatem rather poignantly explains that her agenda "represented a third route to change, which explored the internal transformation or reform of the political, economic, and social institutions of Islamic society before years of colonial modernization effectively foreclosed that alternative" (196).

In *The Mirror of Contemplation*, Taymur wrote a feminist allegory revolving around economic power. A lion loses his authority over a lioness, which hunts and takes care of her family independently; free from economic slavery, she is no longer obligated to obey him (al-Id 14). Taymur was at the forefront of Arabic writers who discussed the relationship between power, economics and gender in the framework of the emancipation of women.

In *The Mirror of Contemplation*, she cunningly challenged the premise that public debate should be an exclusively male dominion. Whereas Fawwaz may have used caustic language, Taymur utilized the language of men to refute their sway in their own territory. Her approach was novel. She highlighted the profound shifts taking place within the family and proposed answers to the issues posed by wholesale, willy-nilly Western-style modernization. Hatem asserts that, "for the first time during that century a woman initiated a public discussion about gender roles and rights emerging as an independent agent of women who were not simply its discursive object" (197).

Hatem also points out that, as distinct from other women writers who focus on domesticity, Taymur's work redefined women's interests by engaging with a wide spectrum of economic, political and religious issues. As long as she remained in her place and did not extend too far into the male domain, her male contemporaries were content to praise her work (197). However, with her interpretation of religious texts to suggest that men's domination is contingent and their familial leadership is conditional rather than absolute, she went too far and "there was a united male effort to stop her" (197).

She had provoked wrath and hostility amongst both men and women, resulting in efforts by her sons to punish her for attempting to expand women's liberties, as well as vicious and debilitating accusations that she was responsible for the death of her beloved daughter Tawhida through neglect of her family duties. Her love poetry provoked allegations that she was having an *affaire*. Despite her problematic relationships with women during this period, Taymur fostered solidarity amongst women who were attempting to transgress patriarchal boundaries (198).

Taymur's use of the thousand-year old *maqamah* form[7] may have helped to pigeonhole her writing as being essentially old-fashioned (the work is variously and awkwardly entitled, in English as *The Consequences of Circumstances in Words and Deeds* and *The*

---

[7] A prosimetric form, in which rhymed prose is alternated with poetry, and which displays great rhetorical skill. A study by Ailin Qian in comparative literature may be of interest: "The Maqamah as Prosimetrum: A Comparative Investigation of its Origin, Form and Function."

Consequences of Changing Speech and Practice.) Elsadda cites May Ziyada's somewhat facile description of this work: "Like any respectable traditional story, this one has a king, a prince, a vizier, and a boon companion" (105). However, the deployment of traditional aesthetics and use of archetypical figures should not relegate Taymur's work to that of chiefly historical interest.

The autobiographical tensions inherent in Taymur's love poetry and the disciplinary measures to which she was subjected by male family members are echoed today in the reception and criticism of Arabic women writers. Taymur tried to dampen speculation about autobiographical elements in her amorous poetry by saying that she was simply exercising her pen; even today, it is not always easy for women to dismiss suspicions of immorality when writing about subjects deemed to be immoral. While men authors may be subjected to similar scrutiny and a conflation of their personal integrity and fictive writing, women, burdened with conflicting obligations and pressures relating to perceived virtue or honor and freedom of expression, have found themselves at the center of accusations and fallacious attacks that would be considered irrelevant for most men (the personal attacks on Nabokov over *Lolita* being perhaps a notable exception).

That Taymur inspired and even helped to launch the careers of many women writers is indisputable; that she may form part of the heritage of modern writers—both male and female—is less understood. This is in part due to a misreading of her work and perhaps in larger part to gender inequality. Few would seriously contend that Shakespeare and Dickens were not potent inspirations for G.K. Chesterton, for example. Although Chesterton's writing does not imitate or even resemble that of his literary heroes, the lineage is perceptible and readily acknowledged. This book suggests that Taymur, Hashim, Fawwaz and other notable women writers should take their rightful place in the galaxy of literary lights that have exerted lasting influence on, and provided inspiration for, generations of writers.

Opening New Spaces

May Ziyada (1886 – 1941) is included here because of an interesting innovation that she applied to a venerable form. She wrote biographies not only of Aisha Taymur but also of Malak Hifni Nasif (who wrote under the pseudonym Bahithat al-Badiya) and Warda al-Yaziji. May Ziyada's works are of special significance because she mixed biography with autobiography. The addition of her own reflective facets to the gems that she crafted was an original approach. Dwight F. Reynolds demonstrates that Arabic autobiography, "follows no pattern common to western autobiography" and stresses that "fact and specificity" held sway (6).

Story-telling within non-fictional literature, including *adab*,[8] has a long history in Arabic writing, and biography is one of its most important forms—traditionally used as historiography, exemplary literature, and for religious, social, and political education in the development of the cultivated man. Stefan Leder's important work, *Story Telling in the Framework of Non-Fictional Arab Literature* sheds

---

[8] Concepts constituting *adab* are not easy to summarize because they are a vast, wide-ranging field, but include ethical conduct, good manners, and adherence to codes of courtesy governing even such details as posture and gestures. The concepts of refinement and cultural sophistication are also included.

much light on a field that is not as broadly known as it deserves to be amongst the general reading public.

Ziyada opened a space for women in this patriarchal system of inscription and instruction, and by interpolating her personal dimension into an impersonal form may even have opened a space in this *genre* for fictive writing. Arabic learned literature traditionally has a troubled relationship with fiction. Stefan Leder cites G.E. von Grunebaum in pointing out that Arabic literary theory does not provide for fiction, and that, "Fictional narration, where it appears, is imbedded in a mainstream of factual, or allegedly factual, narration" (34). Leder continued:

> The author is generally supposed to render faithfully the account of a witness, and he is thus to be identified with the original narrator. Both author and narrator deliver a report about events from an external point of view. This narrative situation is typical of the constitution of historical narrative, which implies a high degree of factuality .(37)

Julie Scott Meisami takes exception to Stefan Leder's understanding as being Eurocentric (151) and his critique is not accepted here in its entirety.

However, he makes an important point, worthy of consideration. Setting aside the special case of political propaganda, his reading of historical narrative and biography suggests that the inclusion of fiction was regarded as falsehood. This is precisely the spot where Ziyada may have opened a way forward for women writers to question the nature of truth by breaking restrictions and mixing different kinds of truth, some of which were fictional. As Neil Gaiman has one of his characters explain: "Things need not have happened to be true" (12).

Ziyada's imposition of a personal narrator changes the cultural reading of biography and historiography, paving the way for post-modern interpretations of historical narratives as perceptions and manipulations of history rather than as the impartial accounts they were generally supposed to have been. Stefan Leder confirms that, "[t]he absence of a personal narrator who could serve as a focus of the reader's perception is, especially in historical narration, a prerequisite for the construction of tradition from narrative" (38). Ziyada's conflation of biography with autobiography was an important step in women's rewriting of history. Each of the early modern authors mentioned here, and many more, have helped to open the spaces in which modern Arabic women writers make their voices heard.

Chapter Two
Contemporary Arab Women Writers

Modern Times

The progress of modern Arabic women's literature in Egypt, Syria, and Lebanon has not been straightforward. Subject to interruptions caused by conflict and turmoil, control and censorship, physical restrictions on the reproduction of texts, the threat of imprisonment and actual imprisonment, in addition to other forms of both intimate and social repression, such as paternal and familial pressure, literary output has in turn faltered, regressed, and surged forward in unpredictable ways. Al-Id notes that after a promising start in Lebanon, women's writing essentially came to a halt after World War I until the early 1950's (21). Women's writing in Syria was similarly affected. The currents have eddied and flowed, with high and low points in times of both peace and war. At the current moment, the productivity and creativity of Arabic women writers is extraordinary and noteworthy, and yet it remains problematic on many levels, including that of politics in some regions. We will look at Syrian women writers first. Literary connections and correlations abound.

Transitions in Syrian Women's Writing

Some of those connections can be discerned in the work of Widad Sakakini (1913–1991), a Lebanese-Syrian writer who explored women's strength in confronting physical and psychological pain. She touched upon the latent transformations that can be elicited by or generated in the space of transitions created by trauma. Widad Sakakini's novels are worthy of note in this respect, especially *Arwa, Daughter of Woe*.

In their survey of Syrian women writers, Subhi Hadidi and Iman al-Qadi suggest that *Arwa, Daughter of Woe*, published in 1949, is the "first narrative literary work by a woman that can truly be called a novel [in Syria]," and they attribute the ascendance of narrative prose in Syria to the sociological and economic phenomenon of a new and increasing middle class along with the assimilation of Western culture (60). Clearly, by 1949, women had been producing novels for a long time, and there are other factors at play apart from Western influence. Interestingly, in *Doing Daily Battle* when Fatima al-Mernissi spoke of the "terrorist tactics" used to silence her, attribution of her ideas to the West was one of those tactics. Far from silencing women's writing, Hadidi and al-Qadi are appraising it, but even here, the influence of the West is a given.

Women's writing had undergone a long hiatus in both Syria and Lebanon— *Arwa, Daughter of Woe* is the first novel al-Id's research could discover to have been published since before World War I. *Arwa, Daughter of Woe* is foreground in social injustice against a virtuous woman. The protagonist Arwa is a submissive, dutiful wife. While her husband is away on a business trip, his brother makes advances to her, which she rejects. From spite, revenge, anger and humiliation, the brother alleges that she is guilty of adultery; because he is a man, his testimony is accepted. Arwa's harrowing trial results in a sentence of stoning. The sentence is executed, and she is exiled from Damascus.

Arwa is victimized for her differences, and for her beauty and desirability as a sexual object. Arwa pleas: "She wishes that God had created her 'a misshapen, ugly thing that repels the eyes and repulses the heart'" (al-Id 21). Sakakini believed that women were far stronger than portrayed.

> So I took it upon myself to write a novel that would show women's ability to bear pain, which [these male writers] unjustly and falsely claim is antithetical to them. *Arwa bint al-khutub* is a portrait of the slander and abasement that women have endured. In it I gave expression to the way women have suffered from the curse of men and the way their dignity survives in their adherence to piety. (Sakakini cited by al-Id 209)

The rage against men and their contempt and injustice towards women, as expressed in Sakakini's novel, is unusual amongst Syrian writers. Her approximate contemporaries, Colette Khuri and Georgette Hannush, for example, provide more traditional views of women whose lives revolve around men, even though the women characters may be strong, educated and rebellious in the face of societal restrictions. They may criticize the unfaithfulness and arrogance of men, but they do not echo the violence of Sakakini's feelings about the "curse of men".

Narratives of injustice regarding women's chastity and honor are familiar. False accusations of adultery appear in the Hebrew, Greek and Aramaic Bibles (the story of Susanna), and in the Qur'an, hadith and other traditions regarding A'isha, the Prophet's wife. *The Tale of the Pious Man and His Chaste Wife* is "both ancient and widespread" in Arabic and Persian literature (Ulrich Marzolph 1). Shakespeare's Hermione (*The Winter's Tale*) undergoes sixteen years of exile after the unfair trial for adultery in which her accuser is also the judge; Desdemona (*Othello*) pays the ultimate price and Hero (*Much Ado About Nothing*) nearly does so for the arbitrary assault of power against woman's chief asset, her perceived virtue.

As potent and recurrent as the theme is, these earlier stories do not represent the woman's experience of the incidents that unfold in the narrative. We are told that A'isha cried and could not sleep on the night when she learned what people were saying about her, and that Hermione fainted from the shock. We can imagine and to some degree observe the effects of injustice on these women, but the women themselves are rigorously silenced about the dimensions of pain that they experience. They are believed to have violated the most sacred aspect of their existence; while one might expect these women's voices to have been heard, they are now utterly mute.

Women ability to use pain as fuel for change suggests a great strength that is seldom acknowledged as integral to femininity. While Widad Sakakini explores events that are as common in literature as to be almost archetypical, she adopts an atypical point of view, invoking a women's experience of injustice as a form of creative dissidence.

Syrian Resurgence

Just five novels by Syrian women were published in the 1950's; sixteen in the 1960's; thirteen in the 1970's; twenty in the 1980's. Forty novels were published by women in the 1990's. The 1950's enjoyed a surge in the quality of novels, which Subhi Hadidi and Iman al-Qadi attribute to the "greater literary cross-fertilization between Syria and Egypt, Iraq, and the Levant, as well as a flourishing translation movement into Arabic" (64). Notable women writers of the time included Ulfat Idilbi, (1910 or 1912 – 2007) and Salma al-Haffar al-Kuzbari (1923 – 2006). It may be noted that some of what are considered Ulfat Idilbi's best novels were published in the 1990's; a prolific and talented author, she has left a long trail. Amongst others, the young authors In'am Musalima (b. 1938), Colette Suhayl al-Khuri (b. 1937), and Nadiya Khust (b. 1935) were active.

Some writers contend that the notion of "Syrian literature" is oxymoronic and can barely be said to exist, due to the complexities and contradictions inherent in a political, national and individual identity in the circumstances of colonial occupation, migration, the redrawing of borders, and exile. Bifurcated or ambiguous identity is, of course, a common aspect of human experience, but may be uncommonly complex in the case of Syrians.

Edward Said reflected a good deal on identity and famously asserted that he was the last Jewish intellectual; he wrote eloquently about his identification with Palestine as a place, an idea, a loss, and a longing. May Ziyada was Palestinian-Lebanese, and arguably, Egyptian. Even Nadiya Khust's "Syrianness" is rendered more complex by displacement and destruction. Her *Exodus from Paradise* is full of yearning and lament for the loss of the Old City, Damascus, and what that might mean for future generations.

A Cry for Freedom – Syrian Progressions

"As to the critic who finds it difficult to pinpoint my writing in one area, I will make things easy for him. He can write on the drawer in

which he files my work, 'a cry for freedom!'" (Samman, in *Al Ittihad* interview n. pag.).

Legitimate critique of literature requires some understanding of its context. Samman's cry for freedom arrived against a background of women writers who were consistently perpetuating traditional gender roles in their writings. That is not to suggest that all Syrian women writers were directly or indirectly sustaining the very institutions that repressed them. However, the study of Syrian writers performed by Hadidi and al Qadi indicates that, even where women struggled with socio-cultural norms that refused them the opportunity to make choices and obliterated their individuality, they hesitated to experience themselves as *becoming*, as ambiguous, changing, evolving persons. They underwent pain and misery—even to the point of self-destruction—but failed to confront the sublime. Their constructs of themselves as being incomplete without a man, with their needs and identities secondary to and contingent upon a man's, rendered them psychologically unprepared to face the transformation, in-betweenness and transcendence that can result from coming face-to-face with extremes of pain, love, terror, and beauty.

In her works on consciousness and experience in Islamic philosophy, Anna-Teresa Tymieniecka suggests that the consequences of the stagnation of women's development as humans add yet another layer of suffering to their lives. "Not only our being, but all being is

becoming in Tymieniecka's view. All being engages in ontopoiesis—
in making itself through the process of transcending itself, reaching
out towards a world" (Kathleen Haney 84).

Two examples will suffice, *Damascus Bitter Sweet* and *Zayna*.
Published in 1980, Ulfat al-Idilbi's *Damascus Bitter Sweet* features a
protagonist who is intelligent and educated and who participates in
political activism against French colonialism, yet is entirely wrapped
up in man and family. Not merely an old-fashioned tragic romance,
the work both reflects and affects the prevailing value system; its
hero "sees her entire existence as dependent" on her lover. She
must adjust herself to his needs and interests (Hadidi and al-Qadi
82). She is not a whole being unto herself; beingness is incomplete
without a man, and questions relating to becoming hardly arise.

It is not easy to determine precisely how the taste and mores of
readers shaped *Damascus Bitter Sweet*, and how the book helped to
shape popular opinion. It seems reasonable to suppose that al-
Idilbi's readers felt sympathy for and some commonality with the
protagonist. Mona Mikhail notes that "[p]opular culture has long
been considered a reliable source for understanding society", which
offers a key reason as to why this study focuses on books that have
been widely read (11). The protagonist is victimized by her brother,
who has murdered her lover to prevent her from marrying beneath
her class. She decides to end her life because she "sees her

continued existence as a betrayal of her lover; with him gone, so is her reason to live" (Hadidi and al-Qadi 82).

A decade later (in 1990), Wisal Samir published *Zayna*, in which the protagonist's dependence on a man is as strong as ever. Her mother advises her to be utterly subservient to her husband, advice unchanged for untold generations: "We learned in our lives not to resist the husband, not to wrong him even if he wrongs us. The husband … is a little god." As in earlier books, the stunting of women's human development is preserved and enforced by the deeply entrenched patriarchal system as well as by women.

Samman's Western education has provided her with more tools for her writer's toolbox, but they are wielded with Arabic genius and sensibility: "I am influenced by my Western education, but that doesn't mean that I am simply a shadow of it. I am learning how to polish my Arab tools in the light of the literary endeavors of others" (cited by Vinson, n. pag.). The lexicon of magic, dream and animal symbols that she uses, for example, are encoded in Arabic culture.

Surrealism, absurdism and Arab mythology are deftly woven through *The Square Moon, The Swan Genie,* and the Beirut trilogy, *Beirut '75, Beirut Nightmares,* and *Night of the First Billion.* Traditional Arabic archetypes and folkloric characters resurface in her work, transformed but recognizable, in order to signify patterns, manifest the immanent, and give expression to the repressed. Magical symbols, incantations and rituals are, of course, used and practiced in the Middle East for many purposes, including saving a life from illness or violent death, to bind a loved one to a person, and to inflict revenge. The threat of death pervades much of the Beirut trilogy where the supernatural aspect is entirely Arabic in its texture. Dreams are used as a device to explore the outer world of racism, sexism, classism, corruption, and violence, and the inner world of identity and becomingness. Ambiguity and in-betweenness, darkness and fear, injustice and futility are deeply explored in each of the three Beirut volumes, but unlike much absurdist literature, Samman's work is not necessarily nihilist—a thread of hope can be discerned in the fabric of despair.

Sometimes compared with masterpieces such as Balzac's *Lost Illusions* or Flaubert's *A Sentimental Education*, *Beirut '75* is distinctively Arabic. Perhaps one similarity is in the way Samman renders Beirut, once known as the Paris of the Middle East, as a fully rounded character, with an outward show of glamour, beauty and modernity hiding a heart of depravity and sadistic indifference. Flaubert created his own version of Paris as a character, set during the tensions, ideals and betrayals of the revolution of 1830, while Balzac represented a duplicitous Paris in which nothing was as it seemed—and his representation of the provinces is the same; the supposed opposites are united in dissimulation. But Samman carries the hallucinatory, ambiguous, and deceptive nature of

Beirut to far greater extremes. Beirut is Dante's *Inferno*, and all who enter are doomed.

Samira Aghacy highlights how greatly the work of Samman differs from that of many contemporary women writers, who have portrayed Beirut as a straightforward city ripe for liberation from the "...traditional community that is closely aligned with a rural mentality" (503). Without Samman's mordant irony, such characters perceive "the city and the village in ontological opposition between repression and freedom, backwardness and progress, and past and present" (506). Samman vividly depicts the tensions between modernity and tradition, subjugation and autonomy, but without easy answers. Certainly the solution is not to be found in moving from the countryside to the city. *Beirut '75* ends on a sardonically nightmarish note, yet the nightmares may be the very thing that keeps one of the characters from going completely insane amidst the madness in the city. As Homsi reminds us, "[i]n a highly absurdist gesture that combines insight with self-assertion, the novel closes with Farah replacing the placard that announces the entrance to Beirut with a sign that reads: 'Hospital for the Mentally Ill.'" (n. pag.).

Samman once told the *Al Ittihad* newspaper, "Dreams, madness, invocations, and hallucinations are literary tools that help me to probe the depths of humanity" (cited by Homsi, n. pag.). There can be little doubt of the importance of unreality in her work. *Beirut Nightmares*

(*Kawabis Beirut*) juxtaposes menace with the bizarre, fantasy with violence, repetition with unpredictability, all in order to criticize the irrationality, iniquity and idiocy of the war and socio-cultural inequalities. Both dreams and reality itself are nightmares. The characters in the final volume in the trilogy, *Night of the First Billion*, have "fled from the nightmares of their homeland to discover the nightmares of exile," where they continue to experience the socio-cultural and political conditions that they tried to escape by fleeing to Switzerland. This is contrasted with many women writers of the war who have portrayed women as the ones who stayed behind.

Nuha Salib Salibi has written, "Let me die in my country and not suffer the pangs of non-belongingness" (14). Complex and raw, laced with delusions that question the nature of being, becoming and reality, the characters are confronted with the sublime through sign and signified, symbol and deed. The encounter with the sublime is an important motif in the works of Samman. She explores the uncomfortable yet liberating space in between dualities. Such in-betweenness implies the immense potential of becomingness, even while many of her characters seem to have no choice but to go to their doom. Her sophisticated use of dreams, myths and the surreal, along with a relative, contingent sense of that which is supposed to be immutable, such as right and wrong, truth and fantasy, place her in the top tier of post-modern authors of any culture, not only those who write in Arabic.

Women in War — Lebanese Progressions

As in Syria, the production of novels in Lebanon after World War I went into steep decline. Layla Ba'lbakki's (b. 1934) *I Live*, published in 1958, was controversial for its use of the first-person, which gave women a distinctive, individual and overt voice. Allen states that Ba'lbakki's work is a challenge, because, "[t]he account of family relationships and feelings is no longer given within the framework of a distant, omniscient third-person narrative, but shifts to a direct first-person experiential montage" (104).

The Lebanese civil war (1975 – 1990) spurred a resurrection in women's writing. Al-Id's study shows that the start of the resurgence could be seen in the 1970's, with works such as *Suicide of a Dead Man* by Hanan al-Shaykh, but a high point was reached in the 1980's, as "writers worked on creating a multi-pronged discourse whose language expressed multiple viewpoints and nuances in diction, mindful of speech variations in a society that was becoming more sharply divided and on the verge of civil war" (30). miriam cooke's discussion of women's writing during the War focuses on a group of writers she identifies as the "Beirut Decentrists" because: "physically, they were scattered all over a self-destructing city; intellectually, they moved in separate spheres" (3).

Khaled M. al-Masri explains the physical, political and socio-economic context for women's Lebanese war writing in order to better understand this important literature, especially the "factors that shape characters' negotiation of sexuality and gender" (14). Lebanon became independent in 1943 and rapidly developed into the glittering gem that Samman treats with such black humor, renowned for its economic robustness and intellectual and cultural freedom. Lebanon was home to some of the most ethnically and religiously varied groups of people anywhere in the world. Approximately 760,000 Palestinians became refugees as a result of the Arab-Israeli War (1948), many of whom fled to Lebanon. Diversity was both strength and weakness, however, and by 1958, serious sectarian strife arose. The matter was more or less settled, but Traboulsi points out that it "was limited to establishing sectarian equilibrium rather than abolishing sectarianism" (140).

The Six-Day War in 1967 destroyed confidence in the Palestinians' ability to regain their home, and brought another flood of Palestinian refugees to Lebanon. Just three years later, the Jordanian army killed over 3000 Palestinians and the PLO moved its base to Lebanon, "further complicating the delicate balance between the country's many different factions" (al-Masri 18). Traboulsi paints a grim picture of squalid living conditions, gross inequalities, social disorder, and the absence of essential infrastructure and services that contributed to a lack of allegiance towards the government as the country edged towards open conflict: "on the eve of the war, there were between 40,000 and 50,000 empty luxury apartments in Beirut alone, while successive waves of migrants from the rural areas crammed into shantytowns and squats and ravaged entire suburbs" (160).

Fragmentation and Loss

Fragmentation and division was both a physical and psychological fact of the Lebanese civil war, effectively preventing the process of fully being and becoming; women's paths to transition and self-realization were further complicated. The Green Line dividing Beirut along essentially Muslim East and Christian West was a potent symbol in Etel Adnan's (b. 1925) *Sitt Marie Rose*, published in 1978. Marie Rose is a Christian, who teaches deaf-mute Muslim children and crosses the Green Line because, as she tells the militia who indict and try her: "I don't consider the Palestinians an enemy. They belong to the same ancestral heritage the Christian party does. They're really our brothers" (54). Her acts inherently threaten the ideology of the Other enforced by the militia, who "execute" (murder) her to prevent her transcendence of their unyielding norms. Her becomingness is perceived as a socio-political menace. Apart from the physical border she has transgressed, she crosses another line: "she was a woman ... mixing in politics, which is normally their [the men's] personal hunting ground" (Adnan 100).

The militias evolved into "sophisticated organized crime networks, participating in arms and drug trafficking, smuggling, outright bank robbery and even piracy" (al-Masri 30). Traboulsi demonstrates that the militia imposed a protection racket on civilians, and perpetuated the war; they became the "crucible in which those sects were reproduced" (230-233). Women tended to write about "dailiness" in the war, "coming to an understanding of their experiences through close examination of the reality they knew best" (cooke 3, al-Masri 25). Daily tragedy, despair, and terror, combined with gender, sex, and class repression to create "psychic fragmentation as well as the elusiveness of truth and reality that are products of the seemingly endless civil war" (al-Masri 28).

In writing about Lebanese war literature, miriam cooke notes that "[w]omen too were beginning to see themselves not as mirrors of the dominant class of men but rather as a self-referential group that had been systematically oppressed" (52). Al-Masri pointed out that the fragmented, postmodern style of writing that reflected the incomprehension, chaos, disconnection and loss related to the war appeared in both men's and women's writing, but that women's writing tends to be unrecognized while the works of two male writers in particular are generally regarded as seminal. Elias Khoury's 1977 *Little Mountain* and Rashid al-Daif's 1983 *The Obstinate* and 1986 *Passage to Dusk* exemplify the nightmarish, surreal, absurd, and multiple voices and conflicting narratives often found in the writing of the Lebanese civil war. "The external violence of the war and its internalization, expressed in nightmares, become indistinguishable" (cooke 33).

If ontopoiesis is a profound human need, it must make itself manifest, and indeed the urgency towards becomingness finds a way around the fragmentation produced by the war. Aggression, increased independence, and confusion created new paths towards becoming. miriam cooke writes of a Lebanese war character, "[s]he was passing from passivity to consciousness and rejection of what was formerly unquestionable. She was becoming the center, the self, in contrast with whom the men were the periphery, the other" (135).

The complex negotiations between sexuality, gender and violence are other fields for confrontations with the sublime and awakening in-betweenness and potential for transcendence. Evelyne Accad suggests that women's writing uniquely exposes gender repression in war novels, as their characters,

[R]ealize that their oppression is strongly tied to their sexuality and gender roles and tend to seek alternatives in nonviolent personal and social engagements, whereas male writers and protagonists continue to reinforce the patriarchal order and practice acts of revenge and violence (al-Masri 44).

Such realizations open the path for transformation, or at least greater subjectivity and knowing, deliberate choices, which might have been otherwise impossible.

Egyptian Progressions

Unlike Syria and Lebanon, Egypt saw significant literary production by women between the World Wars. Suhayr al-Qalamawi's 1935 publication of *My Grandmother's Stories* contrasted the past, present and future, using the ancient Arabic framing technique to set the grandmother's stories within another story. The grandmother may bewail the decay of morality, chastity and dignity that accompanies modernization, but at the same time the author suggests that in the confrontation between old and new, the new will ultimately prevail. Elsadda sees Suhayr al-Qalamawi's writing as trying "to represent reconciliation instead of conflict" (114).

As a nexus of power relationships, the fallen woman is of strong interest to Arabic women writers. While she is, at times, completely victimized and outcast from society, at other times she is both victim and victimizer, exploited and exploiter. In 1944, 'A'isha 'Abd al-Rahman (Bint al-Shati') published *Lord of the Manor: The Story of a Fallen Woman* concerning a young woman who becomes a pariah, then a saint. Rumors follow her, and she is persecuted wherever she goes, until finally the Bedouin, who know nothing of her background, "see the light of the saints on her face" (cited by Elsadda 115). Speaking of her own experience during 1966-1969, Samman has said:

During those years I confronted others as a foreigner in a foreign land without the protection of family, social status, or money, and I learned what I hadn't known before. The hardest lesson I learned was my final discovery of the superficiality of the bourgeois Damascene society that during those years used to consider me during those years as good as dead – 'a fallen woman' – whereas I was in reality a woman starting to live her life and an artist gaining in awareness. (n. pag.)

An important aspect of 'A'isha 'Abd al-Rahman's work is her highlighting the one-sided imbalance of social mores, our perceptions of identity, being and potential being, and power relationships.

She "questioned the dichotomy of fallen woman/saint, wondering, with the reader, about the moral system that is applied arbitrarily to women and not men" (Elsadda 127). Having already lost her family, friends, social status, and perhaps shelter, comfort, and hope, she has nothing further to lose. Without societal and familial restraints, in a state of liminality, she has achieved a kind of freedom or independence; it is now possible to explore her identity and the process of becoming. Even in the novels where the protagonist knowingly chooses prostitution, the dynamics of power are skewed against her.

Optimism and Failure in Egypt

Elsadda identifies the four important novels published in Egypt in the 1960's as: *The Open Door,* 1960, by Latifa al-Zayyat; *Confessions of a Masculine Woman*, 1960, by Su`ad Zuhayr; *Memoirs of a Woman*

Doctor, 1960, by Nawal El Saadawi; and *Love and Silence,* 1967, by Inayat al-Zayyat (120). Each of these works is a significant marker in the progression of Arabic women's novels in Egypt; however, the scope of this study can permit a glance at only two of the above books, Latifa al-Zayyat's *The Open Door* and el-Saadawi's *Memoirs of a Woman Doctor,* in addition to Alifa Rif`at's quietly radical *View of a Distant Minaret*, published a year before *Woman at Point Zero.*

For about twenty-five years after the publication of *The Open Door*, Latifa al-Zayyat (1923-1996), a major force in Arabic literature, continued to write but refused to publish any more of her work. Elsadda believes that the attempt to understand why Latifa al-Zayyat withdrew from the public sphere as a writer, "may give us the keys that will enable us to approach the concerns of literature in this period, particularly literature by women" (128).

The Open Door is almost painfully optimistic about the potential for personal and women's freedom through active involvement in collective liberation. The story starts with Layla's childhood in the 1940's. She especially experiences otheredness when she leaves childhood behind her. Her father's "traumatised realization" and "hysterical distress" on finding that she was growing up is contrasted with his elated response to his son growing a beard.

As in el-Saadawi's *Memoirs of a Woman Doctor*, Layla's womanhood is regarded only and exclusively as othered; the differences are articulated through the body as the primary manifestation of those differences, and the locus of control and punishment. Layla goes on to have disastrous love affairs, in which her lovers are unfaithful and hypocritical, and to become utterly committed to political activism. Layla is widely considered a semi-autobiographical character. Elsadda cites Latifa al-Zayyat's own powerful and transcendent experience in socio-political participation:

> In the street, I was a fully joined human being, with all my intellectual, emotional, and existential faculties. In the street, I was—we were—re-producing our society. I was us, which was me, and we were crafting tomorrow, feeling it as it took shape and came into being to give voice to the painful contradictions between form and content, image and reality, the conscious, revolutionary intellectual and the false intellectual, enthusiastic slogans and their faulty application, truth and lie .(238)

The circumstances of the 1952 revolution made liberation from imperial repression urgent, followed by liberation from monarchical despotism. For the greater good, it was seen as necessary to postpone the struggle for becomingness and women's emancipation, which would naturally follow after collective freedoms had been achieved.

Women in Egypt (and Algeria and elsewhere) are still being asked to sacrifice their need for personal freedom to nationalistic goals. El-Saadawi has explicitly rejected this approach, in the belief that freedom is unattainable without the liberation of women. Al-Zayyat, however, embraced altruistic objectives at great cost to herself. She confessed that this "imposed schizophrenia" had deep ramifications: "Others respected me, and I had to pay for this respect. In the sense of controlling my personal, emotional needs. I had to pay..." (cited by Pascale Ghazaleh n. pag.). After contributing so enthusiastically and significantly to the betterment of all, the failures of the movement she tried to advance left her embittered and disillusioned, unwilling to participate further in the public realm— even to publish her writing.

> Her writing after *The Open Door* no longer reflects overriding confidence, where merging with the collectivity, the moment "I" is submerged into "we," is the moment of true freedom—to give voice to the painful contradictions between form and content, image and reality, the conscious, revolutionary intellectual and the false intellectual, enthusiastic slogans and their faulty application, truth and lie .(Elsadda 128)

The experience of a strongly united group and the fervor of collective good as something greater than oneself may be a form of the sublime, in which a sort of transcendence is possible.

However, the failure of the group seemed to invalidate the experience and especially the potential for full becomingness, so that al-Zayyat retreated. The group itself became a focus of repression, in that it was unacceptable to criticize it. Repulsed and disappointed by what she had become, she was forced to withdraw from socio-political activities and concentrate on herself for her own survival. Pascale Ghazaleh quotes al-Zayyat in an interview: "I... relaxed, for a time, in my private life. I indulged in my private affairs. ...I stopped working for what I believed to be right" (n. pag.).

Pascale Ghazaleh emphasized the conflict between her own needs and the greater good of the group during a period of idealism and the potential to perform acts of historical importance. "El-Zayyat was scarred by the impossibility of reconciling her own desires and the reality of which she was a part. To resolve this dilemma, she may have believed it necessary to annihilate her own individuality..." (n. pag.). Paradoxically, the disintegration or destruction of identity, always painful, can be followed by the joy of discovery and transformation, the construction of a new identity.

This becomingness is central to Arabic women's writing. Elsadda proposes that the reasons that led al-Zayyat to "imprison her writings" still influence women writers "of certain political affiliations," rendering an understanding of her distorted experience of becomingness and the sublime, and consequent silence, important even today (128). It is also possible that al-Zayyat's experience helps to illuminate the absence of some writers from official politics; for example, Nawal el-Saadawi has never joined a political party, although she considered running for president in 2005 (Malti-Douglas 8).

Al-Zayyat began writing *The House Owner* in 1962, but she only completed and released it in 1994, "weighting it with the depth of experience and insight acquired with the passing of time" (Elsadda 130). Importantly, al-Zayyat only discussed the necessity of becomingness, after she realized that she had spent her life "striving for the absolute and that the absolute is the spouse of death. I realize that there is no permanency and no stability in a life, the nature of which is perpetual change" (83). Her acceptance of change and becoming, rather than attempting to achieve and maintain a state of being, is a signal of al-Zayyat's maturity.

Memoirs of a Woman Doctor

In the author's note to a recent edition of *Memoirs of a Woman Doctor*, el-Saadawi discussed her relationship with the book:

> I still consider *Memoirs* like a first daughter, full of youthful fervor and expressing a reality which is still relevant today. It is a simple, spontaneous novel in which there is a lot of anger against the oppression of women in my country, but also a great deal of hope for change, for wider horizons and a better future .(iv)

The story begins with a statement about the narrator's tense and troubled relationship with her femininity. As with *Woman at Point Zero*, the female body is central to the text. "But the body in the Saadawian literary corpus is more than a source of conflict. It is intimately tied to a discourse of gender and sexual definition" (Malti-

Douglas 7). El-Saadawi made this clear: "The struggle between me and my femininity began very early…before my femininity sprouted and before I knew anything about myself, my sex, or my origin…indeed, before I knew what hollow had enclosed me before I was tossed out into this wide world (1).

As in Latifa al-Zayyat's *The Open Door*, the protagonist's deficiencies are contrasted with her brother's perfections. As will be discussed shortly, the brother-sister relationship in Arab families can be very distinct from and problematical in different ways to that in Western families. "And there was only one meaning for the word 'girl' in my mind…that I was not a boy…I was not like my brother…" (11). The many freedoms her brother enjoys offers denigrating comparisons, with little hope of ever overcoming her faults, in that all criticisms of her are based on her not being a boy. "My brother goes out in the street to play, without permission from my mother or my father, and returns at any time…but I, I do not go out without permission. … I must watch my every movement…I must hide my desire for food and so I eat slowly and drink soup without a sound…" (12).

In *Woman at Point Zero*, food would be a critical symbol of the most basic control over the hero's every move. Even in *Memoirs*, food plays a role in othering the narrator, further defining her limitations and providing a way of exerting bodily control over her. It would be a mistake to think that *Memoirs* is, in fact, autobiographical. Rather, it mimics autobiography to explore some of the issues that recur in el-Saadawi's work, including in *Woman at Point Zero,* in which the first narrator is also a woman doctor.

Medicine seems to interest el-Saadawi in her novels chiefly as a way to reveal social and gendered power structures as they relate to the female body. A prestigious field which a woman has somehow managed to penetrate, the woman doctor uses her privileged (almost masculine) status in unusual ways in her struggle towards becomingness. Venturing beyond womanly confines, she extends her being into in-between or ambiguous spaces until she can discover her true identity and construct a new life. El-Saadawi sometimes uses highly confrontational or traumatic incidents to trigger the transitions and becomingness in her characters.

Egyptian Women Writer's Explorations of Self

Born just one year before el-Saadawi, Fatimah Rif`at (1930-1996) too, was unafraid of tackling the degradation and pain of "female genital mutilation, forced marriage, rural marriage traditions such as the ritual of declaring and proving the bride's virginity and the family's honor", as well as women's unfulfilled sexuality (Elsadda 124). Unlike el-Saadawi, however, Rif`at was denied the education she desired—she wanted to attend the College of Fine Arts and instead was obliged to enter an arranged marriage. Initially, in the years between 1955 and 1960, her husband allowed her to write, but even though she used the pseudonym Alifa Rif`at, her work was too unsettling, too challenging. He threatened divorce if she continued. She acquiesced, and remained silent and frustrated until she started publishing again in 1974 (in contrast, el-Saadawi divorced two husbands rather than give up writing).

Rif`at's stories, set mainly in the provincial environment, are forthright, yet evocative, condemnations of women serving men's selfish pleasures, and their own repressed sex drive. Although she wrote frankly of women's lack of fulfillment, women are subservient—her stories are imbued with a Muslim *ethos*, firmly entrenched in patriarchal values even while protesting their effects on women. Leila Ahmed noted that the works of Rif`at and el-Saadawi come from two different veins of thought on bodies and sexuality, two entirely different world views (41). Rif`at's voice is scandalous, but not radical. Like el-Saadawi, she explores Freudian repression, and the effects of authoritarianism. Her treatment of the transformative power of female sexuality was bold in its social context.

Sometimes the lack of emotion and what is not said is more expressive than a dramatic scenario. One of Rif`at's stories, *Distant View of a Minaret*, begins with a husband and wife having sex. The husband disregards her except when he wishes to fulfill his needs. After years of having been denied sexual release, she no longer feels desire; the wife is submissive, disengaged, emotionally uninvolved.

The call to prayer absorbs her attention, and she feels a greater connection with that call than with her husband. Her husband dies abruptly, but the apathy, stagnation and emotional suppression that have been enforced on her for her entire life are so strong that she feels little or nothing concerning his passing.

The wife's psychological blockage has resulted in numbness towards life; she has no outlet other than the religious faith that sustains her. Mona Eltahawy's point of view on the sublimation through prayer depicted in this story is interesting but requires a somewhat dismissive attitude towards Islamic faith that many women will not share. More important is Rif`at's daringly explicit depiction of the neglect of and disdain for women's sexual and emotional needs, one of the first. Rif`at says a great deal in a compact, subtle, and sparing manner.

Often, Rif`at seems to have more in common with the early women novelists than the outstanding later voices. However much her characters may be resigned or resentful, she embraces a paradigm in which men are strong and women are weak; a man is the sun around which a woman's universe revolves. Mutiny against arranged marriages, teenage pregnancy, and female genital mutilation is permitted, but not rebellion against the social and religious order that forms the structure of patriarchy. However, sometimes Rif`at extends beyond her own self-imposed limits. Another of her stories, published in 1983, offers outspoken approach to repressed desire, magical realism, and mixture of dream and myth with the mundane. It also draws inevitable comparisons to one of Aphra Behn's adroitly ambiguous works.

The delicately-nuanced *My World of the Unknown* (`Alami al-majhul) is narrated in the first person, making the intimate story more immediate. She travels to a small town to search for a home, because her husband's government job has transferred to that location. She is almost hypnotized by an abandoned farmhouse on a canal that looks like one from her recurring dreams, and feels strongly that she must live in that house, despite a warning that local people believe it to be inhabited by a spirit and the efforts of a young women who is squatting in the house to make her leave.

One day she sees a strangely intoxicating sight— an enormous, dazzlingly attractive snake. She is euphoric. Initially frightened by her own awakening sexuality, she tells her husband what she has seen. He boards up the chink the snake has used, neatly symbolizing his role in her life. A local sheikh tells her that the snake is a blessing as it is really one of the monarchs of the earth. In her physical and emotional isolation, the snake begins to dominate her thoughts and fantasies. It opens an ecstatic new world for the wife—a world that has been there all along, but utterly repressed and with no hope of fulfillment through her husband. She commences a passionate affair with the snake spirit:

I felt her as she slipped between the covers, then her two tiny fangs,
like two pearls, began to caress my body; arriving at my thighs, the
golden tongue, like an arak twig, inserted its pronged tip between
them and began sipping and exhaling; … and all the while the
tenderest of words were whispered to me as I confided to her all my
longings .(Rif'at 73)

A virtually universal mythological symbol, the snake is redolent of
ancient ritual and belief. Biblical imagery and Freudian theories are
suggested.

It may be noteworthy that Aphra Behn used the snake in her poem
*To the Fair Clarinda, Who made love to me / Imagin'd more than
woman*. Behn also uses the snake as a phallic symbol, but one which
is wielded and possessed by a woman. Clarinda seductively
combines masculine and feminine elements; she is woman, but
more than woman. She is both Hermes and Aphrodite, and
commands the love, fascination and fantasies of the writer. The
hierarchy of gender is overturned, rendered meaningless in the face
of such gendered complexity. Rif`at's parable also features unusually
direct sensuality, longing, and gender complications.

While obviously Freudian, the parable also seems to suggest that we
conspire with our oppressors to deprive ourselves of the fulfillment
of our deepest needs; as the affair progresses, the wife's well-being
increases. The snake guides her through indescribable joy and
beauty in the hidden worlds of the spirit. The snake-spirit's

tenderness, consideration and love are a revelation for her. Her ready response to the snake's enchantment shows how little her husband cherishes her more clearly than any complaint.

Somewhat paradoxically, the snake spirit tells her that there is no sin, as they are now married. There is also no sin because they are both female. Unlike her contemporaries such as el-Saadawi, Rif`at is careful not to violate Quranic injunctions. However, both have written about the connection between terror and desire in the encounter with something perceived as greater than oneself, or the confrontation with the sublime.

> At last the cool touch withdrew, leaving me exhausted. I went into a deep slumber to awake at noon full of energy, all of me a joyful burgeoning to life. Curiosity and a desire to know who it was seized me again. I looked at the corner of the wall and found that the hole was wide open. Once again I was overcome by fear. I pointed out the crack to my husband, unable to utter, although terror had once again awakened in me passionate desire .(Rif'at 73)

The emotionally and sexually deprived wife finds the love for which she has hungered, and her relationship with the snake spirit easily eclipses that with her husband.

The affair lasts for months. Yet on some level, it seems that she cannot quite allow herself to keep enjoying such unearthly, secret bliss, or to enjoy a new state of being. For the first time, she is in a position to taste profound personal change, perhaps even transcendence. The fact that she is able to touch and feel something of the unknowable through magical or supernatural means foregrounds the metaphysical character of her experiences. She is on the verge of transcending the identity that has been constructed for her by a patriarchal society and discovering who she really is. Rather than brave the metamorphosis and undergo the discomfort of the unknown, the ambiguous and the in-between during the process, she abandons the discovery of her true self and returns to the carefully, systematically constructed self she knows so well. "I am frightened that I shall feel that I am tumbling down into a bottomless pit and being destroyed" (75).

Her husband brings an abrupt and violent end to the idyll by killing the snake. What the spirit leaves behind is an ugly, blackened thing of a body. Joy, beauty and the door to self-knowledge vanish, and the dreamlike quality of the narrator's life is shattered by the desecration. The husband has violated the pact of the djinn, and she and her family are no longer welcome in that house. Her encounters with the sublime—heights of beauty, love, and knowledge, terror, rapture and torments of a desire that she could barely have imagined—are not quite enough to persuade her to accept her genuine self.

Her rejection of herself as a fully realized being, inculcated virtually from birth by familial, social and cultural norms, is passive; it is her husband who commits the final transgression, permanently closing the door on her *becomingness*. However passive she may be, she is also a participant in that act of destruction, because her husband's action is predictable. She had known what he would do if he saw the snake. She never takes action to move beyond the status quo in her life; she may desire and long for her djinn lover, but the opportunity is lost.

Georg Lukács stresses that, "The disintegration of personality is matched by a disintegration of the outer world" (23-25). This disintegration may be frightening to contemplate; Rif`at's hero is not equipped to deal with it. Not only her inner world but also her outer one would have needed to undergo intense change if she had been able fully to confront the sublime.

Chapter Three
Intercultural and
Inter-Traditional Understanding

De-Westernizing Feminist Critique

...for the novel form is, like no other, an expression of this transcendental homelessness.

~Georg Lukács, *The Theory of the Novel*

Rightly or wrongly, it has been broadly accepted in much writing on modern Arabic literature that the novel itself is a Western import. Thus, why not apply Western values and theories to the evaluation of Arabic women's novels? It may be easier to accept wholly and superficially the notion of Western importation when there is a foundational belief that Arabic culture is based on the assimilation of influences (Persian, Hellenic, etc.) rather than the creation and production of its own culture. In this view of culture as a one-way flow of culture from the West to the Arabic world, the foundation stone for the essentially derivational quality of the culture was laid long ago: Arab civilization arose amongst desert tribesmen who themselves created and innovated little, but were exposed to the great achievements of the Persians, Babylonians, Indians and Greeks, from which the heights of Arabic culture are derived.

There are many problems with this view. Fundamentally, it begs the question: how did remote, backward desert dwellers manage to produce extremely high quality translations of the most important, key texts in their fields? From the earliest dates of recorded history, they were able to discern the difference between, for example, Euclid and erroneous imitators in geometry, mathematics, astronomy and other fields. They transmitted and taught only the most accurate texts. Their ability to select correct ancient texts (and improve them through research conducted at universities such as Baghdad) is generally glossed over in the quick character sketch of Arabic culture that seems to inform and constitute the subtext of both Western and many Arabic texts. The high level of innovation, enquiry, and creativity encountered in Arabic culture is often as much ignored as the unique textures and backgrounds of Arabic writing, in all of its confounding; contradictory diversity. This is being rectified with new scholarship, of course, but perhaps the mainstream press is not quite up-to-date.

While this researcher does not advocate using Western criteria for Arabic women's novels, such criteria are not necessarily invalid approaches provided their limitations are discussed and understood. The application of Western feminist or other grounds for criticism as though such criteria are universal is, of course, disturbing and can result in distortion. However, it would seem drastic to discard the entire body of Western feminist research, critique and writings—and the majority *are* Western. It can be expected that in time, imbalances will be righted and greater number of studies, observations and theories will be collected in different socio-cultural environments.

A single example may suffice. Psychoanalytic theories form a respected basis for studying novels and other cultural productions. However, there may be insufficient scientific bases to suppose that some of Freud's (and subsequently-developed) theories apply as readily to the childhoods of Arab (or Chinese or Polynesian) people as to those brought up in a Western European setting. Indeed, some conjectures on the difficult relationship between brother and sister in Arabic culture have suggested that this relationship contains deep-seated and far-reaching psychological dilemmas analogous to but not identical with the Oedipus Complex.

Hasan El-Shamy dubbed the brother-sister dynamics that develop in specifically Arabic family conditioning the "The Brother-Sister Syndrome." This matter is highly contentious, yet may well inform certain aspects of the twin brother-sister relationship in el-Saadawi's *The Circling Song*—perhaps more comprehensible, nuanced and insightful to an Arab audience than to an audience unfamiliar with these sibling dynamics, which differ deeply from the sibling rivalry familiar to a Western audience.

Indeed, Sigmund Freud and Otto Rank, in the fourth and revised edition of *Die Traumdeutung* [*The Interpretation of Dreams*], which, incidentally, discusses the issues of sibling rivalry in connection with fairy tales, see the literary input of childhood as a definite source for dreams and the psyche and therefore, according to this, it would be different if you are told different stories (402). There is much to understand about how stories within our own culture can affect us—both Freud and Jung analyzed fairy tales and Bruno Bettelheim's work on the meaning and importance of such stories remains important.

Even the venerable death drive and pleasure principle may be given a different interpretation in an Arabic context. For example, Anastasia Valassopoulos, drawing on the work of Jean Laplanche regarding the combination/unification of the death drive and sex drive, persuasively argues that, for deeply oppressed Arab women, sex may be associated with the death drive, while death (or rather, profound danger and threat of death) may trigger the pleasure principle, although it is further complicated by being bound up in masochism and narcissism (55-75).

Valassopoulos' analysis is placed in the framework of the Lebanese war, but may well extend beyond those borders. In any event, Hasan el-Shamy notes that, "Western terminology, concepts, and diagnostic guidelines dominate Arab psychiatric and psychological theories and practices" and discusses numerous difficulties which may arise from the lack of understanding of Arabic ethno- and socio-cultural differences from Western norms (1). The point here is neither to localize nor to universalize psychoanalytic theory, but simply to problematize assumptions that are taken for granted in the West when applied outside the Western context.

A highly selective eye must to be used in choosing a methodology for analysis that acknowledges and attempts to deal with the complexity and differences even between Arabic women writers from the same country, let alone those from different countries, as well as differences in perception and understanding grounded in even wider cultural divergences amongst the readers of those authors. Mikhail Bakhtin fruitfully explored a reader's dialogic relationship with a text, and a text's ever-changing meanings as it continually undergoes interpretations and reinterpretations. It is the reader who gives meaning to literature, so the dimensions and implications of that literature must always vary over time, from culture to culture, and from individual to individual.

Terry Eagleton refers to Wolfgang Iser's theory of the implied reader: "A work is written for an 'implied reader' who has the correct understanding to make some sense of the subject and language" (73). Eagleton posited that reality was not reflected by language, but produced by it (99). Of course, it is by no means certain that a reader will possess the necessary framework and cultural references to appreciate a foreign work and produce a new reality. Translation is always problematical, but arguably more so for Arab women writers, whose works must often contend not only with contradictory feminist, colonial and post-colonial implications, but also with general ignorance of the culture in which their work is grounded.

Maria Tymoczko posits that, in this case, the translator may be likened to the post-colonial writer, whose metatext is the culture being transmitted. A literary translator is *de facto* concerned with differences not just in language (transposing word for word, mechanically), but with the range of cultural factors that a writer must address when writing to a receiving audience composed partially or primarily of people from a different culture. The culture or tradition of a post-colonial writer acts as a metatext which is rewritten—explicitly and implicitly, as both background and foreground—in the act of literary creation (21).

Since we have moved into an age of more or less instant global communication, it may be more imperative than ever before to evaluate literary works in ways that have the potential to bring new understandings and new realities to a readership from broadly disparate backgrounds. That is not to suggest that refined and localized readings would not offer great richness; they may well provide deeper, more nuanced and more widely differing understandings of the works so studied.

This researcher argues that many Western methodologies are appropriate, and none should be rejected merely because of origin. Given the quantity and quality of intercultural relations, the fact that a theory, whether psychoanalytic, feminist or otherwise, may be "tainted" with Westernness should not in itself render it ineligible as a methodology. The sophisticated cultural productions of Arabic women writers can stand up well to any reasonable basis for analysis, but more appropriate methodologies will give far more useful and meaningful results.

Critiquing Arabic Women Writers

Some special criticisms seem to be reserved for Arabic women writers, for example, those who supposedly bring Arab or Islamic society into disrepute by revealing patriarchal forms of oppression and playing into the stereotypes of the West. As Malti-Douglas points out, "[n]o one accuses the leftist writer who denounces the upper classes or political despotism of giving the Arabs a bad name" (9). This effort to silence women has a long and hoary history; Malti-Douglas links its implications to outright censorship, which forecloses a reasonable engagement with the literature being criticized:

> Another fallacious concept underpinning attempts to deal with (or avoid dealing with) the problematic fiction of Arab women writers is exemplified by the following response to the work of el-Saadawi: The Egyptian physician, polemicist and authoress [sic] Nawal al-Saadawi has several works in English translation: some of these are extended in length and partly imaginative and are therefore considered to be novels. These include *Woman at Point Zero; God Dies by the Nile; Two Women in One; Memoirs of a Woman Doctor; The Fall of the Imam*; and *The Circling Song*. In each case these works combine autobiographical references and personal opinions with fictional representations of persons either real or imagined in a radical feminist context with heavily emotional, anti-establishmentarian and anti-Islamic overtones. They are highly controversial in the Arab world .(45)

Here, the insinuation of trivial literary value renders it unnecessary to deal with the issues raised in the six works named, as if the denial of literary legitimacy can also deny the profound and highly charged questions posed in Saadawi's work.

If el-Saadawi's books were less emotional, less anti-establishmentarian and less anti-Islamic, would it be acceptable to connect with and discuss the emotional, socio-political and religious concerns in her books? Malti-Douglas shows that this dismissiveness is not a one-off, but is repeated in different ways. Other Arabic authors make light of el-Saadawi's craft and openly regret her fame in the West. "Sabry Hafez, speaking of *Memoirs of a Woman Doctor* and *The Fall of the Imam*, writes: 'I hesitate to call them novels.' One could ask: if they are not novels, what are they? What the critic is really trying to do, of course, is to call into question their literary worth." The works of men writers may be subjected to all manner of criticisms, but it is not a common tactic to call into question whether their books qualify as novels in order to be engaged with at an intelligent level.

Extending the Horizon

It is notoriously difficult to evaluate modern art in a balanced, unbiased manner, whether writing, painting, architecture, or any other contemporary form of creative expression. Often, we are too close in time and prejudice to assess modern works accurately— praise may be fulsome and criticism egregious. Therefore, in this book, we have started from the foundation of a brief overview of the origins of the Arabic novel in order to problematize and decenter the almost invariable supposition that the novel is a Western import, with all of the unspoken colonialist implications of that assumption.

Further, we have reviewed some of the relevant progressions of women's writing in Egypt, Syria, and Lebanon. It must be acknowledged that such geographic delineations are to some extent arbitrary and do not reflect the political realities that have resulted in exile, diaspora and fragmentation. Transnational migration has far-reaching implications for women, beyond those of identity and homelessness: Lynn Stephen and Geraldine Pratt, amongst others, have performed admirable studies of the economic and class ramifications of exodus.

The intent of examining trends and currents in Arabic women's writing is to place the origin of these writings within their socio-political, cultural, artistic and intellectual horizons. Engagement and dialogue with both a foreign tradition and one's own can be deepened through what Hans-Georg Gadamer terms "effective historical consciousness" (75). In Gadamer's view, a person does not ordinarily rise beyond their traditional prejudices when interpreting a text. As Abdul Rahim Afaki explains: "It is in the living process of tradition that we acquire our prejudices and fore-meanings regarding a text..." (198). When the text is within our own culture, we are inside it—it is everywhere around us. "Everywhere" gives us no place from which to view.

Afaki discusses Gadamer in the context of the limitations of Western hermeneutics when it comes to understanding transitions in Islamic thought: "we are always within the situation, and the 'illumination' of it is a task which 'cannot be completely achieved,' as we exist as historical beings, and all of our knowledge 'proceeds from what is historically pre-given'" (200).

Gadamer, Bakhtin and others have treated intercultural and inter-traditional understanding rather thoroughly. It is, however, relevant to acknowledge that, while historicity has limits in its approach to understanding a text, a review of the origin of the novel, of Arabic women's writing, may broaden the horizon. Afaki defined the horizon as "the range of vision that includes everything that can be seen from a particular vantage point," with the added advantage that, through historicity, one can better understand the relative significances of all that is encompassed in the horizon, "whether it is near or far, great or small" (200).

Effective historical consciousness makes it possible for the present horizon to meet the historical horizon. The longer and wider view accommodates greater appreciation of the cultural productions of one's own and other traditions; however, a historicity may give rise to other and further understandings. One of the key points that both Gadamar and Afaki make about the horizon is that we cannot see past it. "Our prejudices ... determine the hermeneutical situation in which we find ourselves. On the other hand, they constitute the horizon of a particular present, for they represent that beyond which it is impossible to see" (202).

Thus, increasing historical understanding may imply an ever-widening hermeneutic circle, opening the possibility of a "fusion of horizons of the two traditions which enables one to make the meaning understandable in one's own life-world which is at first linguistically foreign and unintelligible" (Afaki 202). While they are both very useful tools, it may be noted that neither an historical nor a linguistic approach can fully illuminate a text.

Bibliography

Chapter One

Abu-Haidar, Farida. A Voice from Iraq: The Fiction of Alia Mamdouh. *Women: A Cultural Review*. 9;3. 1998. pp 305–11. Print.

Accad, Evelyne. "Gender and Violence in Lebanese War Novels." *From Patriarchy to Empowerment: Women's Participation, Movements, and Rights in the Middle East, North Africa and South Asia*. Syracuse: Syracuse University Press, 2007. 293-310. Print.

Ahmed, Leila. Arab culture and writing women's bodies. *Gender Issues*, 9;1, 1989. pp. 41-55

Al-Id, *Yumna*. Lebanon. *Arab Women Writers: A Critical Reference Guide 1873-1999*. The American University in Cairo Press: Cairo. 2008. pp.13-59. Print.

Allen, Roger. *An Introduction to Arabic Literature*. Cambridge: Cambridge University Press. 2000. Print.

—. *The Arabic Novel: An Historical and Critical Introduction*. Syracuse: Syracuse University *Press*, 1995. Print.

—. "The Mature Arabic Novel Outside Europe." In *Modern Arabic Literature*. Badawi, M.M. (Ed). Cambridge: Cambridge University Press. 1992. pp. 192-222. Print.

—. (Ed). *Essays in Arabic Literary Biography: 1850-1950.* Harrassowitz: 2010. Print.

Al-Shaykh , Hanan. The New Shahrazad. *Sweet Briar College World Writers Series.* 2000. http://gos.sbc.edu/a/al-Shaykh .htm Last accessed 19 May 2012. Web.

Azadpur, Mohammad. *Reason Unbound: On Spiritual Practice in Islamic Peripatetic Philosophy.* SUNY. 2011. Print.

Booth, Marilyn. *May Her Likes Be Multiplied: Biography and Gender Politics in Egypt.* University of California Press. 2001. Print.

—. Exemplary Lives, Feminist Aspirations: Zaynab Fawwāz and the Arabic Biographical Tradition. *Journal of Arabic Literature* 26; 1/2. 1995.pp 120-146. Print.

El-Saadawi, Nawal. "Towards a Strategy for Incorporating and Integrating Arab Women in the Arab Nationalist Movement." *Conference Papers.* Beirut: Center for Arab Unity Studies,. 1982. pp 471-91.

Foucault, Michel. Discipline *and Punish: The Birth of the Prison*, trans. A. Sheridan, Harmondsworth: Peregrine, 1977. Print.

Gaiman, Neil. *The Sandman, Dream Country.* New York: DC Comics. 1991. Print.

Grace, Daphne M. Arab women Write the Trauma of Imprisonment and Exile. *Arab Women's Lives Retold: Exploring Identity Through Writing.* 181- 200. Syracuse University Press: New York. 2007. Print.

Hadidi, Subhi and Iman al-Qadi. Syria. *Arab Women Writers: A Critical Reference Guide 1873-1999*. The American University in Cairo Press: Cairo. 2008. pp.60-97. Print

Hafez, Sabry. Intentions and realisation in the narratives of Nawal El-Saadawi. *Third World Quarterly*, 11;3. p. 188-198. 1989. Taylor & Francis, Ltd. Web. http://www.jstor.org/stable/3992625

Hatem, Mervat T. *Literature, Gender, and Nation-Building in Nineteenth-Century Egypt: The Life and Works of `A'isha Taymur*. Palgrave Macmillan. 2001. Print.

Leder, Stefan ed. Story-Telling in the Framework of Non-Fictional Arabic Literature. Wiesbaden: Harrassowitz. 1998. Print.

Lewis, Reina and Nancy Micklewright. *Gender, Modernity and Liberty: Middle Eastern and Western Women's Writings, a Critical Sourcebook*. I.B.Tauris: 2006. Print.

Meisami, Julie Scott. Narrative and Meaning in Medieval Muslim Historiography. *On Fiction and Adab in Medieval Arabic Literature*. Ed. Philip F. Kennedy. Wiesbaden: Harrasowitz Verlag. 2005. Print.

Mikhail, Mona. *Seen and Heard A Century of Arab Women in Literature and Culture*. Olive Branch Press: Northampton, Massachusetts. 2004. Print.

Moosa, Matti. *The Origins of Modern Arabic Fiction.* Lynne Rienner Publishers Inc; 2nd ed. 1997. Print.

Rastegar, Kamran. Literary *Modernity between the Middle East and Europe: Textual transactions in nineteenth-century Arabic, English, and Persian literatures.* London and New York: Routledge. 2007. Print.

Reynolds, Dwight F., editor *Interpreting the Self: Autobiography in the Arabic Literary Tradition.* Berkeley: University of California Press, 2001.

Sawicki, J., 'Feminism and the Power of Discourse' in J. Arac (ed.) *After Foucault: Humanistic Knowledge, Postmodern Challenges,* New Brunswick and London: Rutgers University Press, 1988. pp. 161-178. Print.

Shaaban, Bouthaina. Preparing the Way: Early Arab Women Feminist Writers. *Al Raida.* XX; 100. 2003 10-14. Web.

Valassopoulos, Anastasia. *Contemporary Arab Women Writers: Cultural Expression in Context.* London and New York: Routledge. 2007. Print.

Wayne, T.K. *Feminist Writings from Ancient Times to the Modern World: A Global Sourcebook and History.* Santa Barbara, California: Greenwood, an imprint of ABC-CLIO. 2011. Print.

Yuval-Davis, Nira. *Gender and Nation.* London: Sage Publications, 1997.

Zeidan, Joseph. *Arab Women Novelists: The Formative Years and Beyond.* State University of New York Press. 1994. Print.

Chapter Two & Chapter Three

Adnan, Etel. *Sitt Marie Rose*. 1978. Print.

Aghacy, Samira. Lebanese Women's Fiction: Urban Identity and the Tyranny of the Past. Studies. <in "International Journal of Middle East Studies" 33/04. 2001. pp. 503-523. Print.

Ahmed, Leila. Arab culture and writing women's bodies. *Gender Issues*, 9;1. 1989. pp. 41-55. Print.

Al-Id, *Yumna*. Lebanon. *Arab Women Writers: A Critical Reference Guide 1873-1999*. The American University in Cairo Press: Cairo. 2008. pp.13-59. Print.

Allen, Roger. *An Introduction to Arabic Literature*. Cambridge: Cambridge University Press. 2000. Print.

—. *The Arabic Novel: An Historical and Critical Introduction*. Syracuse: Syracuse University *Press*, 1995. Print.

—. "The Mature Arabic Novel Outside Europe." In *Modern Arabic Literature*. Badawi, M.M. (Ed). Cambridge: Cambridge University Press. 1992. pp. 192-222. Print.

—. (Ed). *Essays in Arabic Literary Biography: 1850-1950*. Harrassowitz: 2010. Print.

Al-Masri, Khaled M. *Telling Stories of Pain: Women Writing Gender, Sexuality and Violence in the Novel of the Lebanese Civil War*. 2010.

al-Shaykh , Hanan. The New Shahrazad. *Sweet Briar College World Writers Series*. 2000. http://gos.sbc.edu/a/*al-Shaykh* .htm Last accessed 19 May 2012. Web.

Al-Zayyat, Latifa. *The Open Door,* trans. Marilyn Booth, Cairo: AUC Press, 2000. Print.

Azadpur, Mohammad. *Reason Unbound: On Spiritual Practice in Islamic Peripatetic Philosophy*. SUNY. 2011. Print.

Booth, Marilyn. *May Her Likes Be Multiplied: Biography and Gender Politics in Egypt.* University of California Press. 2001. Print.

—— Exemplary Lives, Feminist Aspirations: Zaynab Fawwāz and the Arabic Biographical Tradition. *Journal of Arabic Literature* 26; 1/2. 1995. pp.120-146. Print.

cooke, miriam. *Dissident Syria: Making Oppositional Arts Official..* Durham: Duke University Press, 2007. Print.

—— Women Write War: The Feminization of Lebanese Society in the War Literature of Emily Nasrallah. *Bulletin (British Society for Middle Eastern Studies)* 14;1. 1987. pp 52-67..

El Saadawi, Nawal. "Towards a Strategy for Incorporating and Integrating Arab Women in the Arab Nationalist Movement." *Conference Papers*. Beirut: Center for Arab Unity Studies,. 1982. pp 471-91.

Elsadda, Hoda. Egypt. *Arab Women Writers: A Critical Reference Guide 1873-1999*. Cairo: The American University in Cairo Press.. 2008. pp 98-161. Print.

Foucault, Michel. Discipline *and Punish: The Birth of the Prison*, trans. A. Sheridan, Harmondsworth: Peregrine, 1977. Print.

Ghazaleh, Pascale. Eyes Wide Open. *Al-Ahram Weekly*. 520. 8 - 14 February 2001. Cairo. Print and Web.

Hadidi, Subhi and Iman al-Qadi. Syria. *Arab Women Writers: A Critical Reference Guide 1873-1999*. The American University in Cairo Press: Cairo. 2008. p.60-97. Print

Hafez, Sabry. Intentions and realisation in the narratives of Nawal El-Saadawi. *Third World Quarterly*, 11;3. p. 188-198. 1989. Taylor & Francis, Ltd. Web. http://www.jstor.org/stable/3992625

Haney, Kathleen. Lukacs, Georg. *The Theory of the Novel*. London: The Merlin Press Ltd. 1978. Print.

— *The Meaning of Contemporary Realism*, trans. by John & Necke Mander. London: Merlin Press. 1963. Print.

Marzolph, Ulrich. "Crescentia's Oriental Relatives: The "Tale of the Pious Man and His Chaste Wife" in the Arabian Nights and the Sources of Crescentia in Near Eastern Narrative Tradition." Marvels & Tales 22.2 (2008). Web.

Malti-Douglas, Fedwa. *Men, Women, and God(s): Nawal El Saadawi and Arab Feminist Poetics*. Berkeley: University of California Press. 1995. Print.

Mikhail, Mona. *Seen and Heard A Century of Arab Women in Literature and Culture.* Olive Branch Press: Northampton, Massachusetts. 2004. Print.

Rifaat, Alifza. Distant View of a Minaret: And Other Stories. Oxford: Heinneman Educational Publishers. 1987. Print.

Sakakini, Widad. *Shawk fi-l-hasid fi-l-naqd wa-l-adab.* Damascus: Arab Writers' Union, 1981. Print.

Salibi, Nuha Salib. *From under the debris: a personal viewpoint.*

Samman, Ghada. *Al Ittihad* interview. Web.

Traboulsi, Fawwaz. An Intelligent Man's Guide to Modern Arab Feminism. *Al-Raida*. XX; 100. 2003. 15-19. Web.

Tymieniecka, Anna-Teresa. Reason, Spirit and the Sacral in the New Enlightenment: Islamic Metaphysics Revived and Recent Phenomenology of Life. Springer. 2001. Print.

Tymoczko, Maria. Post-colonial Writing and Literary Representation. *Post-Colonial Translation: Theory and Practice*, Susan Bassnett and Harish Trivedi eds. London: Routledge. 1999. Print.

Vinson, Pauline Homsi. Ghada Samman: A Writer of Many Layers. *Al Jadid Magazine.* 8;39. Spring 2002. Print.